Born in 1985

by

Kerry Butters.

Born in 1985

Millennium: **2nd millennium**

Centuries: 19th century – **20th century** – 21st century

Decades: 1950s 1960s 1970s – **1980s** – 1990s 2000s 2010s

Years: 1982 1983 1984 – **1985** – 1986 1987 1988

1985 (MCMLXXXV) was a common year starting on Tuesday (dominical letter F) of the Gregorian calendar, the 1985th year of the Common Era (CE) and *Anno Domini* (AD) designations, the 985th year of the 2nd millennium, the 85th year of the 20th century, and the 6th year of the 1980s decade. The year **1985** was designated as the *International Youth Year* by the United Nations.

Contents

- 1 Events
- 2 Births
- 3 Deaths
- 4 Works of Fiction taking place in 1985
- 5 Nobel Prizes
- 6 In the News

Events

January

- January 1
  - The Internet's Domain Name System is created.
  - Greenland is withdrawn from the European Economic Community.
  - First UK Cellular Mobile Phone Network Launched by Vodafone
- January 7 – Cellnet Launches 2nd UK Cellular Network
- January 10 – Kenya recognizes the Sahrawi Arab Democratic Republic (SADR).
- January 15 – Tancredo Neves is elected president of Brazil by the Congress, ending the 21-year military rule.
- January 17 – British Telecom announces it is going to phase out its famous red telephone boxes.
- January 20 – U.S. President Ronald Reagan is privately sworn in for a second term in office (publicly sworn in, January 21).
- January 27 – The Economic Cooperation Organization (ECO) is formed.

- January 28 – In Hollywood, the charity single "We Are the World" is recorded by USA for Africa.

February

- February 4 – The border between Gibraltar and Spain reopens for the first time since Francisco Franco closed it in 1969.
- February 5 – Australia cancels its involvement in U.S.-led MX missile tests.
- February 9 – U.S. drug agent Kiki Camarena is kidnapped and murdered in Mexico (his body is discovered March 5)
- February 10 – Nelson Mandela rejects an offer of freedom from the South African government.
- February 12 – Rafael Addiego Bruno is sworn in as interim President of Uruguay.
- February 14 – CNN reporter Jeremy Levin is freed from captivity in Lebanon.
- February 16
  - Israel begins withdrawing troops from Lebanon.
  - The ideology of Hezbollah is declared in a "program" issued in Beirut.
- February 19
  - William J. Schroeder becomes the first artificial heart patient to leave hospital.
  - China Airlines Flight 006 is involved in a mid-air incident; while there are 22 minor injuries and 2 serious injuries, no one is killed.
  - The first episode of the long-running British soap opera *EastEnders* is broadcast on BBC One television.
- February 20 – Minolta releases the Maxxum 7000, the world's first autofocus single-lens reflex camera.

- February 28 – 1985 Newry mortar attack: The Provisional Irish Republican Army carries out a mortar attack on the Royal Ulster Constabulary police station at Newry, killing 9 officers in the highest loss of life for the RUC on a single day.

March

- March – The *GNU Manifesto*, written by Richard Stallman, is first published.
- March 1 – After a 12-year-long dictatorship, Julio María Sanguinetti is sworn in as the first democratically elected President of Uruguay.
- March 3 – An 8.0 on the Richter magnitude scale earthquake hits Santiago and Valparaíso, Chile, leaving 177 dead, 2,575 injured, 142,489 houses destroyed, and about a million people homeless.
- March 4 – The United States Food and Drug Administration approves a blood test for AIDS, used since then to screen all blood donations in the United States.
- March 8 – A Beirut car bomb, planted in an attempt to assassinate Islamic cleric Sayyed Mohammad Hussein Fadlallah, kills more than 80 people, injuring 200.
- March 11
  - Mikhail Gorbachev becomes General Secretary of the Soviet Communist Party and *de facto* leader of the Soviet Union.
  - Mohamed Al-Fayed buys the London-based department store company Harrods.
- March 14 – Five lionesses at the Singapore Zoo are put on birth control after the lion population increases from 2 to 16.
- March 15 – Vice-President José Sarney, upon becoming vice president, assumes the duties of president of Brazil, as the

new president Tancredo Neves had become severely ill, the day before. Sarney will become Brazil's first civilian president in 21 years, upon Neves' death on April 21.

- March 16 – Associated Press reporter Terry Anderson is taken hostage in Beirut (he is released on December 4, 1991).
- March 17 – Expo '85, a World's Fair, is held in Tsukuba, Ibaraki, Japan, until September 16.
- March 18 – Australia's longest running soap opera *Neighbours* debuts on Seven Network.
- March 21 – Canadian paraplegic athlete and activist Rick Hansen sets out on his 40,000 km, 26 month Man in Motion tour which raises $26M for spinal cord research and quality of life initiatives.
- March 23 – OCAM is dissolved.
- March 24 – United States Army military intelligence officer Arthur D. Nicholson is shot by Soviet military sergeant Aleksandr Ryabtsev at a Soviet military base in Ludwigslust, East Germany.
- March 25 – The 57th Academy Awards are held in Los Angeles, with *Amadeus* winning Best Picture.
- March 31 – WrestleMania debuts at Madison Square Garden.

April

- April 1
  - Two Japanese government-owned corporations, Nippon Telegraph and Telephone Public Corporation, and Japan Tobacco and Salt Public Corporation, are privatized and change their names to Nippon Telegraph and Telephone, and Japan Tobacco.

- Eighth seeded Villanova defeats national powerhouse Georgetown 66–64 to win the first 64 team field NCAA Tournament in Lexington, Kentucky.
- April 10
  - Madonna launches her Virgin Tour, her first concert tour, in New York City.
- April 11
  - The USS *Coral Sea* collides with the Ecuadorian tanker ship *Napo* off the coast of Cuba.
  - First Secretary Enver Hoxha, leader of the People's Socialist Republic of Albania dies.
- April 12 – El Descanso bombing: A terrorist bombing attributed to the Islamic Jihad Organization in the *El Descanso* restaurant near Madrid, Spain, mostly attended by U.S. personnel of the Torrejón Air Base, causes 18 dead (all Spaniards) and 82 injured.
- April 15 – South Africa ends its ban on interracial marriages
- April 19 – The Soviet Union performs a nuclear test in eastern Kazakhstan.
- April 21 – Brazilian President Tancredo Neves dies, he is succeeded by Vice President José Sarney. The Vice President post is left vacant until 1990.
- April 23 – Coca-Cola changes its formula and releases New Coke (the response is overwhelmingly negative, and the original formula is back on the market in less than 3 months).
- April 28 – The Australian Nuclear Disarmament Party (NDP) splits.

May

- May 4 – The 30th Eurovision Song Contest takes place in Gothenburg, Sweden and is won by the Bobbysocks! song *La det swinge* for Norway.
- May 5 – U.S. President Ronald Reagan joins West German Chancellor Helmut Kohl for a controversial funeral service at a cemetery in Bitburg, West Germany, which includes the graves of 59 elite S.S. troops from World War II.
- May 11
  - The FBI brings charges against the suspected heads of the 5 Mafia families in New York City.
  - Fire engulfs a wooden stand at the Valley Parade stadium in Bradford, England, during a football match, killing 56.
- May 13
  - Philadelphia Mayor Wilson Goode orders police to storm the radical group MOVE's headquarters to end a stand-off. The police drop an explosive device into the headquarters, killing 11 MOVE members and destroying the homes of 61 city residents in the resulting fire.
  - The National Assembly of Kuwait grants women the right to vote. The right is revoked in 1999 and re-instated in 2005.
- May 15
  - An explosive device sent by the Unabomber injures John Hauser at University of California, Berkeley.
  - Argentinian President Raúl Alfonsín terminates Argentinian administration of the Falkland Islands but

does not relinquish the Argentinian claim over the islands.
- May 16 – Scientists of the British Antarctic Survey announce discovery of the ozone hole.
- May 19 – John Anthony Walker Jr. is arrested by the FBI for passing classified naval communications to the Soviet Union.
- May 23 – Thomas Patrick Cavanaugh is sentenced to life in prison for attempting to sell stealth bomber secrets to the Soviet Union.
- May 25 – Bangladesh is hit by a tropical cyclone and storm surge, which kills approximately 10,000 people.
- May 29 – Heysel Stadium disaster: 38 spectators are killed in rioting on the terraces during the European Cup final between Liverpool F.C. and Juventus at Heysel Stadium in Brussels, Belgium.
- May 31 – Forty-one tornadoes hit Ohio, Pennsylvania, New York and Ontario, killing 77.

June

- June 6 – The remains of Josef Mengele, the physician notorious for Nazi human experimentation on inmates of Auschwitz concentration camp, buried in 1979 under the name of Wolfgang Gerhard, are exhumed in Embu das Artes, Brazil.
- June 13 – In Auburn, Washington, police defuse a Unabomber bomb sent to Boeing.
- June 14
  - TWA Flight 847, carrying 153 passengers from Athens to Rome, is hijacked by a Hezbollah fringe group. One

passenger, U.S. Navy Petty Officer Robert Stethem, is killed.

- ○ The Schengen Agreement is signed between certain member states of the European Economic Community, creating the Schengen Area, a bloc of (at this time) 5 states with no internal border controls.
- June 15 – Studio Ghibli, an animation studio, is founded in Tokyo.
- June 17 – John Hendricks launches the Discovery Channel in the United States.
- June 23 – Air India Flight 182, a Boeing 747, is blown up by a terrorist bomb 31,000 feet (9,500 m) above the Atlantic Ocean, south of Ireland, on a Montreal–London–Delhi flight, killing all 329 aboard.
- June 24 – STS-51-G: Space Shuttle *Discovery* completes its mission, best remembered for having Sultan bin Salman Al Saud, the first Arab and first Muslim in space, as a Payload Specialist.
- June 25 – Irish police foil a Provisional Irish Republican Army–sponsored 'mainland bombing campaign' which targeted luxury vacation resorts.
- June 27 – U.S. Route 66 is officially decommissioned.

July

Live Aid at JFK Stadium in Philadelphia

- July 1 – The Convention on the Transfer of Sentenced Persons enters into force.
- July 3 – *Back to the Future* opens in American theatres and ends up being the highest-grossing film of 1985 in the United States and the first film in the successful franchise.
- July 4 – Ruth Lawrence, 13, achieves a first in mathematics at Oxford University, becoming the youngest British person ever to earn a first-class degree and the youngest known graduate of Oxford University.
- July 10 – The Greenpeace vessel *Rainbow Warrior* is bombed and sunk in Auckland Harbour by French DGSE agents.
- July 13
    - *Live Aid* pop concerts in London and Philadelphia raise over £50 million for famine relief in Ethiopia.
    - U.S. Vice President George H. W. Bush serves as Acting President for 8 hours, while President Ronald Reagan undergoes colon cancer surgery at Bethesda Naval Medical Center in Bethesda, Maryland.
- July 19
    - U.S. Vice President George H. W. Bush announces that New Hampshire teacher Christa McAuliffe will become the first schoolteacher to ride aboard the Space Shuttle *Challenger*.
    - The Val di Stava Dam in Italy collapses.
- July 20 – State President of South Africa, P. W. Botha, declares a state of emergency in 36 magisterial districts of South Africa amid growing civil unrest in black townships.
- July 23 – Commodore launches the Amiga personal computer at the Lincoln Center in New York.
- July 24 – *The Black Cauldron* makes its theatrical debut.

- July 31 – Liberia recognizes the Sahrawi Arab Democratic Republic (SADR).

August

- August 2 – Delta Air Lines Flight 191 crashes near Dallas, Texas, killing 137 people.
- August 7 – Takao Doi, Mamoru Mohri and Chiaki Mukai are chosen to be Japan's first astronauts.
- August 12 – Japan Airlines Flight 123 crashes in Japan, killing 520 people (the worst single-aircraft disaster in history).
- August 14 – The Accomarca massacre takes place in Ayacucho, Peru.
- August 15 – Three miners die in an accident at a coal mine in southeastern Kentucky.
- August 20 – Iran–Contra affair: The first arms, 96 BGM-71 TOWs, are sent to Iran in exchange for hostages in Lebanon and profits for the Nicaraguan Contras. The public does not know about the arms sale.
- August 22 – British Airtours Flight 28M: The 737's left engine catches fire while on its take off roll, 55 people are killed while trying to evacuate the aircraft.
- August 25 – Samantha Smith, 13, "Goodwill Ambassador" between the Soviet Union and the United States for writing a letter to Yuri Andropov about nuclear war, and eventually visiting the Soviet Union at Andropov's request, dies in the Bar Harbor Airlines Flight 1808 plane crash.
- August 28 – The first smoking ban banning smoking in restaurants in the United States is passed in Aspen, Colorado.

- August 31 – Richard Ramirez, the serial killer known as the Night Stalker, is captured in Los Angeles.

September

- September 1 – The wreck of the RMS *Titanic* (1912) in the North Atlantic is located by a joint American-French expedition led by Dr. Robert Ballard (WHOI) and Jean-Louis Michel (IFREMER) using side-scan sonar from RV *Knorr*.
- September 2 – Hurricane Elena makes landfall on the U.S. Gulf Coast after reaching a Category 3 status
- September 6 – Midwest Express Airlines Flight 105, a Douglas DC-9, crashes just after takeoff from Milwaukee, killing 31.
- September 11 – Pete Rose becomes the all-time hit leader in Major League Baseball, with his 4,192nd hit at Riverfront Stadium in Cincinnati.
- September 13
  - Super Mario Bros. is released for the Nintendo Entertainment System.
  - Steve Jobs resigns from Apple Computer in order to found NeXT.
- September 19 – An 8.1 Richter scale earthquake strikes Mexico City. Around 10,000 people are killed, 30,000 injured, and 95,000 left homeless.
- September 20 – The capital gains tax is introduced to Australia.
- September 22 – The Plaza Accord is signed by 5 nations.
- September 23 – Italian crime reporter Giancarlo Siani is killed by Camorra.

- September 28 – Brixton riots are sparked with the shooting of Dorothy 'Cherry' Groce by the Metropolitan Police in Brixton, an area of south London, England.

October

- October 1 – The Israeli air force bombs PLO Headquarters near Tunis.
- October 3 – The Space Shuttle *Atlantis* makes its maiden flight.
- October 4 – The Free Software Foundation is founded in Massachusetts, USA.
- October 7 – The cruise ship *Achille Lauro* is hijacked in the Mediterranean Sea by 4 heavily armed Palestinian terrorists. One passenger, American Leon Klinghoffer, is killed.
- October 18 – The first Nintendo home video game console in the United States is released as the Nintendo Entertainment System.

An CIE 141 Class about to haul the rolling stock forward for the NIR Class 111 to shunt into position at Dublin Connolly to bring the Enterprise back to Belfast Central.

November

- November 5 – In an all-English match, Mark Kaylor defeats Errol Christie to become the middleweight boxing champion, after the two brawl in front of the cameras at the weigh-in.

- November 9 – In an all-Soviet match, 22-year-old Garry Kasparov defeats Anatoly Karpov to become the youngest-ever undisputed winner of the World Chess Championship.
- November 12 – A total solar eclipse occurs over Antarctica at 14:11:22 UTC.
- November 13 – Armero tragedy: The Nevado del Ruiz volcano erupts, killing an estimated 23,000 people, including 21,000 killed by lahars in the town of Armero, Colombia.
- November 18
  - The comic strip *Calvin and Hobbes* debuts in 35 newspapers in the United States.
  - Elmo is first introduced by name on the children's TV show Sesame Street.
- November 19 – Cold War: In Geneva, U.S. President Ronald Reagan and Soviet Union leader Mikhail Gorbachev meet for the first time.
- November 20 – Microsoft Corporation releases the first version of Windows, Windows 1.0.
- November 23 – EgyptAir Flight 648 is hijacked by the Abu Nidal group and flown to Malta, where Egyptian commandos storm the plane; 60 are killed by gunfire and explosions.
- November 25 – 1985 Aeroflot Antonov An-12 shoot-down: A Soviet Aeroflot Antonov An-12 cargo airplane, en route from Cuito Cuanavale to Luanda, is shot down by South African Special Forces and crashes approximately 43 km east of Menongue, the provincial center of the Cuando Cubango Province, Angola, killing 8 crew members and 13 passengers on board.

- November 26 – U.S. President Ronald Reagan sells the rights to his autobiography to Random House for a record US$3 million.
- November 29 – Gérard Hoarau, exiled political leader from the Seychelles, is assassinated in London.

December

- December 1
  - The Organization of Ibero-American States for Education, Science and Culture (Organización e Estados Iberoamericanos para la Educación la Ciencia y la Cultura) (OEI) is created.
  - The Ford Taurus and Mercury Sable are released for sale to the public.
- December 8 – The South Asian Association for Regional Cooperation (SAARC) is established.
- December 12 – Arrow Air Flight 1285, a Douglas DC-8, crashes after takeoff from Gander, Newfoundland, killing 256, 248 of whom were U.S. servicemen returning to Fort Campbell, Kentucky from overseeing a peacekeeping force in Sinai.
- December 16 – In New York City, Mafia bosses Paul Castellano and Thomas Bilotti are shot dead in front of Spark's Steak House, making hit organizer John Gotti the leader of the powerful Gambino crime family.
- December 20 – Pope John Paul II announces the instituting of World Youth Day for Catholic youths.
- December 24 – Extremist David Lewis Rice murders civil rights attorney Charles Goldmark as well as Goldmark's wife and two children in Seattle. Rice suspects the family of

being Jewish and Communist and claims his dedication to the Christian Identity movement drove him to the crime.

- December 27
  - Rome and Vienna airport attacks: Abu Nidal terrorists open fire in the airports of Rome and Vienna, leaving 18 dead and 120 injured.
  - American naturalist Dian Fossey is found murdered in Rwanda.
- December 31 – American singer, songwriter and actor Ricky Nelson dies in a plane crash in De Kalb, Texas.

Date unknown

- The Australian state of Victoria celebrates its 150th anniversary.
- Harold Kroto, Robert Curl and Richard Smalley discover C_{60}, a type of fullerene.
- Western Sahara is admitted to the Organization of African Unity; Morocco, which claims Western Sahara, leaves in protest.
- Solarquest, the space age real estate game, is first published by Golden.
- ATI Technologies is founded.
- The Tommy Hilfiger brand is established.
- DNA is first used in a criminal case.
- Multiple cases of espionage in the United States prompt the media to label this "The Year of the Spy".
- Africa has a population growth of 3.2 percent per year.
- The Asian tiger mosquito, an invasive species, is first found in Houston, Texas.
- The Famine in Ethiopia continues; USA for Africa ("We Are the World") and Live Aid raise funds for famine relief.

- The Fall of Communism begins with resistance gaining victory in the Democratic Republic of Afghanistan. Over the next six years, other countries begin renouncing Communism, ending with the collapse of the Soviet Union in 1991.

Births

January

Lewis Hamilton

András Kállay-Saunders

Kalomira

- January 1
    - Jeff Carter, Canadian hockey player
    - Steven Davis, Northern Irish footballer
- January 2
    - Teng Haibin, Chinese gymnast
    - Heather O'Reilly, U.S. women's national soccer player
- January 3
    - John David Booty, American football quarterback, USC
    - Linas Kleiza, Lithuanian basketball player
- January 4
    - Danielle Campo, Canadian Paralympic swimmer
    - Lenora Crichlow, British actress
    - Al Jefferson, American basketball player
    - Fernando Rees, Brazilian race car driver
- January 5
    - Lopez Lomong, Sudan-born American Olympic runner
    - Diego Vera, Uruguayan footballer
    -

- January 7
  - Lewis Hamilton, British Formula One driver
  - Tiger Kirchharz, German dancer
  - Wayne Routledge, English Footballer
- January 8 – Rachael Lampa, American Christian singer
- January 9 – Bobô, Brazilian footballer
- January 11
  - Newton Faulkner, British musician
  - Rie fu, Japanese singer and songwriter
  - Lucy Knisley, American comic artist and musician
- January 15 – Brandon Mebane, American football player
- January 16
  - Joe Flacco, American football player
  - Gintaras Januševičius, Lithuanian pianist
  - Siddharth Malhotra, Indian actor
  - Amy Manson, Scottish actress
- January 17
  - Kangin, Korean singer (Super Junior)
  - Simone Simons, Dutch singer
- January 19
  - Damien Chazelle, American film director and screenwriter
  - Rika Ishikawa, Japanese singer and host of television and radio programs
- January 20 – Marina Inoue – Japanese voice actress
- January 21
  - Aura Dione, Danish singer-songwriter
  - Sasha Pivovarova, Russian model
- January 22
  - Akira Nagata, Japanese singer (Run&Gun), actor and voice actor

- - Orianthi, Australian guitarist and singer
- January 23 – Doutzen Kroes, Dutch supermodel
- January 25
  - Tina Karol, Ukrainian singer
  - Michael Trevino, American actor
- January 26
  - Edwin Hodge, American actor
  - Rusko, British musician
- January 28
  - J. Cole, American rapper, singer and record producer
  - Tom Hopper, English actor
  - András Kállay-Saunders, Hungarian American recording artist, songwriter and record producer
- January 29
  - Bosh Berlin, American drummer (Living Things)
  - Liu Chunhong, Chinese weightlifter
  - Marc Gasol, Spanish basketball player
  - Isabel Lucas, Australian actress
  - Jessica Marais, Australian actress
- January 30 – Richie Porte, Australian professional cyclist (Tasmanian)
- January 31 – Kalomira, Greek American singer

February

Cristiano Ronaldo

Trevor Smith

Yulia Volkova

Haylie Duff

- February 2 – Fontel Mines, American football player
- February 4
  - Bashy, English recording artist and actor
  - Bug Hall, American actor
- February 5
  - Laurence Maroney, American football player
  - Cristiano Ronaldo, Portuguese footballer
  -

- February 6
  - Kris Humphries, American basketball player
  - Joji Kato, Japanese speedskater
- February 7
  - Donald Moatshe, South African musician
  - Tegan Moss, Canadian actress
  - Tina Majorino, American actress
  - Deborah Ann Woll, American actress
- February 8
  - Jeremy Davis, American bassist (Paramore)
  - Bob Morris, American singer-songwriter and guitarist (The Hush Sound)
  - Trevor Smith, Canadian ice hockey player
- February 9
  - David Gallagher, American actor
  - Rachel Melvin, American actress
- February 10 – Anette Sagen, Norwegian ski jumper
- February 11
  - William Beckett, American singer and songwriter
  - Mike Richards, Canadian hockey player
- February 14
  - Karima Adebibe, English actress and model
  - Heart Evangelista, Chinese-Filipino actress
  - Kataxenna Kova, British model
  - Miki Yeung, Hong Kong actress and singer
- February 17 – Anne Curtis, Filipino-Australian actress, television host, model, VJ and singer
- February 18
  - Chelsea Hobbs, Canadian actress and singer
  - Todd Lasance, Australian actor
  - Lee Boyd Malvo, African-American serial killer

- Jos Van Emden, Dutch cyclist
- February 19
  - Haylie Duff, American actress and singer
  - Arielle Kebbel, American model and actress
- February 20 – Yulia Volkova, Russian singer (t.A.T.u.)
- February 21 – Larisa Bakurova, Ukrainian actress and model based in Taiwan
- February 22
  - Hameur Bouazza, Algerian footballer
  - Zach Roerig, American actor
- February 25
  - Benji Marshall, Australian rugby league player
  - Joakim Noah, American basketball player
- February 26
  - Shiloh Fernandez, American actor
  - Miki Fujimoto, Japanese singer
- February 27 – Nicole Linkletter, American model
- February 28
  - Fefe Dobson, Canadian singer
  - Jelena Janković, Serbian tennis player
  - Diego Ribas da Cunha, Brazilian soccer player

March

Kellan Lutz

Jonathan Groff

Keira Knightley

Toby Turner

- March 2
  - Reggie Bush, American football player
  - Robert Iler, American actor
  - Patrick Makau Musyoki, Kenyan long-distance runner
- March 3
  - Alena and Ninel Karpovich, Belarusian twin sister musical duo, members of 3+2
  - Sam Morrow, Northern Irish footballer

- o Nathalie Kelley, Peruvian-born Australian actress
- o Toby Turner, American comedian, actor and YouTuber
- March 4
  - o Scott Michael Foster, American actor
  - o Angela White, Australian pornographic actress
- March 5 – Kenichi Matsuyama, Japanese actor
- March 7 – Cameron Prosser, Australian swimmer
- March 8 – Ewa Sonnet, Polish model
- March 9
  - o Brent Burns, Canadian hockey player
  - o Rachel Nabors, American cartoonist
- March 10 – Lassana Diarra, French footballer
- March 11
  - o Paul Bissonnette, Canadian ice hockey player
  - o Ajantha Mendis, Sri Lankan cricketer
  - o Hakuhō Shō, 69th Yokozuna
- March 12
  - o Lolene, British recording artist and songwriter
  - o Nikolai Topor-Stanley, Australian soccer player
  - o Stromae, Belgian-Rwandan singer-songwriter
- March 13
  - o Hannah Claydon, British bondage model
  - o Emile Hirsch, American actor
- March 14 – Eva Angelina, American pornographic actress
- March 15
  - o Curtis Davies, English football player
  - o Antti Autti, Finnish snowboarder
  - o Eva Amurri, American actress
  - o Kellan Lutz, American fashion model
- March 18
  - o Krisztián Berki, Hungarian artistic gymnast

- o Bianca King, Filipina-Canadian actress and model
- March 19 – E. J. Viso, Venezuelan race car driver
- March 21
  - o Ryan Callahan, American hockey player
  - o Adrian Peterson, American football player
- March 22
  - o Mayola Biboko, Belgian footballer
  - o Jakob Fuglsang, Danish cyclist
  - o Mike Jenkins, American football player
  - o Justin Masterson, American baseball player
  - o Kelli Waite, Australian swimmer
  - o Chris Wallace, American singer-songwriter and producer (The White Tie Affair)
- March 24
  - o Haruka Ayase, Japanese actress and model
  - o Sayaka Hirano, Japanese table tennis player
- March 25 – Carmen Rasmusen, American singer
- March 26
  - o Jonathan Groff, American actor, singer, and dancer
  - o Keira Knightley, English actress
- March 27
  - o Alison Carroll, English actress and model
  - o Danny Vuković, Australian soccer player
  - o Caroline Winberg, Swedish model
- March 28 – Sauli Koskinen, Finnish reality-television star, radio personality and entertainment reporter
- March 29 – William Chak, Hong Kong actor
- March 31
  - o Airi & Meiri, Japanese twin porn actresses and singers
  - o Jessica Szohr, American actress

April

Leona Lewis

Olga Seryabkina

Rooney Mara

Elena Temnikova

- April 1
  - Josh Zuckerman, American actor
  - Daniel Murphy, American baseball player
  - Beth Tweddle, English gymnast
- April 2
  - Barry Corr, Irish footballer
  - Thom Evans, Zimbabwean-Scottish rugby player
  - Stéphane Lambiel, Swiss figure skater
- April 3 – Leona Lewis, English singer
  - Jari-Matti Latvala, Finnish race car driver
- April 4
  - Rudy Fernández, Spanish professional basketball player
  - Ricardo Vilar, Brazilian footballer
- April 5
  - Kim Ji-hoo, South Korean model and actor (d. 2008)
  - Lastings Milledge, American baseball player
- April 6
  - Clarke MacArthur, Canadian ice hockey player
  - Al Mukadam, Canadian actor, director, and producer
  - Frank Ongfiang, Cameroonian footballer

- o Sinqua Walls, American basketball player and actor
- April 7
  - o Ariela Massotti, Brazilian actress
  - o KC Concepcion, Filipina actress and singer
- April 9
  - o Tomohisa Yamashita, Japanese singer and actor
  - o David Robertson, American baseball player
- April 8
  - o Patrick Schliwa, German rugby player
  - o Yemane Tsegay, Ethiopian runner
- April 10
  - o Dion Phaneuf, Canadian NHL hockey player
  - o Wang Meng, Chinese short track skater
- April 12
  - o Hitomi Yoshizawa, Japanese singer and actor
  - o Brennan Boesch, American baseball player
  - o James Alexandrou, English actor
  - o Olga Seryabkina, Russian singer–songwriter (Serebro)
- April 13 – Carmen Carrera, American model
- April 15 – Amy Ried, German pornographic actress
- April 16 – Benjamín Rojas, Argentine singer
- April 17
  - o Jo-Wilfried Tsonga, French tennis player
  - o Luke Mitchell, American actor and model
  - o Rooney Mara, American film and television actress
- April 18
  - o Łukasz Fabiański, Polish footballer
  - o Elena Temnikova, Russian singer (Serebro)
- April 19 – Zhang Xi, Chinese beach volleyball player
- April 22 – Camille Lacourt, French swimmer
- April 23 – Taio Cruz, British singer

- April 24 – Kaori Nazuka, Japanese voice actress and singer
- April 26 – Nam Gyu-ri, Korean singer, former member of SeeYa
- April 28 – Brandon Baker, American actor
- April 30
  - Ashley Alexandra Dupré, American prostitute, R&B singer-songwriter
  - Gal Gadot Israeli actress and model

May

Kyle Busch

Lily Allen

Clark Duke

Carey Mulligan

- May 1 – Drew Sidora, American actress and singer
- May 2
    - Sarah Hughes, American figure skater
    - Kyle Busch, American race car driver
    - Lily Allen, British singer
- May 3 – Meagan Tandy, American actress and model
- May 4 – Bo McCalebb, American/Macedonian basketball player
- May 5
    - Shoko Nakagawa, Japanese actress, voice actress and singer
    - Clark Duke, American actor
- May 6 – Chris Paul, American basketball player
-

- May 9
  - Neha Bamb, Indian actress
  - Chris Zylka, American actor and model
  - Audrina Patridge, American television personality, actress and model
- May 10 – Odette Annable, American actress
- May 12 – Dániel Tőzsér, Hungarian footballer
- May 14
  - Matthew Cardona, American professional wrestler
  - Lina Esco, American actress, producer and activist
  - Dustin Lynch, American country music singer and songwriter
  - Sally Martin, New Zealand actress
- May 15
  - Derek Hough, American dancer and choreographer
  - Cristiane, Brazilian footballer
  - Tyrone Savage, Canadian theatre, film and television actor
- May 17 – Christine Nesbitt, Canadian speed skater
- May 18 – Oliver Sin, Hungarian painter
- May 20 – Chris Froome, Kenyan-born British road racing cyclist
- May 21 – Mutya Buena, British singer and songwriter (of Sugababes)
- May 22
  - Marc-Antoine Pouliot, Canadian ice hockey player
  - Chrissie Chau, Hong Kong model
- May 23 – Kanyeria, Kenyan music producer
- May 25
  - Alexis Texas, American pornographic actress
  - Luciana Abreu, Portuguese singer and actress

- Roman Reigns, American professional wrestler
- May 26 – Ashley Vincent, English footballer
- May 27
  - Chien-Ming Chiang, Taiwanese baseball player
  - Andrew Francis, Canadian voice actor and actor
- May 28
  - Carey Mulligan, English actress
  - Colbie Caillat, American acoustic-folk singer-songwriter
- May 30 – Turk McBride, American National Football League player
- May 31 – Navene Koperweis, American progressive metal musician

June

Bar Refaeli

Dave Franco

Chris Young

Lana Del Rey

Michael Phelps

- June 1 – Ari Herstand, American singer/songwriter
- June 2 – Miyuki Sawashiro, Japanese voice actress
- June 4
  - Evan Lysacek, American figure skater
  - Lukas Podolski, German footballer
  - Ana Carolina Reston, Brazilian fashion model (d. 2006)
  - Bar Refaeli, Israeli model and occasional actress
- June 7
  - Charlie Simpson, English musician
- June 9
  - Sebastian Telfair, American basketball player
  - Sonam Kapoor, Indian actress and model
- June 10
  - Andy Schleck, Luxembuergian road cyclist
  - Rok Perko, Slovenian professional skier
  - Kaia Kanepi, Estonian tennis player
  - Celina Jade, Chinese-American actress
- June 11 – Dmitry Koldun, Belarusian singer
- June 12
  - Tasha-Ray Evin, Canadian singer/guitarist (Lillix)
  - Blake Ross, American software developer

- o Kendra Wilkinson, American model
- o Dave Franco, American television and film actor
- o Chris Young, American country music singer-songwriter
- June 13 – Danny Syvret, Canadian ice hockey player
- June 15
  - o Nadine Coyle, Irish singer (Girls Aloud)
  - o Maxey Whitehead, American voice actress
- June 17
  - o Andrea Demirović, Montenegrin singer
  - o Marcos Baghdatis, Cypriot tennis player
  - o John Gallagher Jr., American actor and musician
- June 19 – Ai Miyazato, Japanese golfer
- June 20
  - o Matt Flynn, American football player
  - o Darko Miličić, Serbian basketball player
  - o Collins Pennie, American actor
- June 21
  - o Kris Allen, 8th American Idol winner, singer-songwriter
  - o Sharna Burgess, Australian ballroom dancer
  - o Lana Del Rey, American singer-songwriter
- June 22
  - o Douglas Smith, Canadian-American actor
  - o Lindsay Ridgeway, American actress
- June 24 – Tom Kennedy, English footballer
- June 25
  - o Annaleigh Ashford, American actress and singer
  - o Ehra Madrigal, Filipina actress
- June 26
  - o Ogyen Trinley Dorje, Tibetan Buddhist spiritual leader

- o Arjun Kapoor, a Bollywood actor
- June 27
  - o Svetlana Kuznetsova, Russian tennis player
  - o Nico Rosberg, German Formula One driver
- June 28 – Phil Bardsley, English footballer
- June 29 – Steven Hauschka, American football player
- June 30
  - o Michael Phelps, American swimmer
  - o Cody Rhodes, American professional wrestler

July

Ashley Tisdale

Chace Crawford

Shantel VanSanten

James Lafferty

- July 1
  - Zohre Esmaeli, Afghan-born fashion model
  - Sebalter, Swiss singer, songwriter and fiddle player
  - Spose, American rapper
  - Léa Seydoux, French actress
- July 2
  - Gábor Máthé, Hungarian Deaflympic Champion in tennis
  - Ashley Tisdale, American actress and singer
  - Corey Bringas American voice actor
- July 3 – Minami Keisuke, Japanese singer and actor
-

- July 5
  - Stephanie McIntosh, Australian actress (Neighbours)
  - Nick O'Malley, British musician (Arctic Monkeys)
  - François Arnaud, French-Canadian stage and film actor
- July 6
  - Matt Overton, American football player
  - Ranveer Singh, Bollywood actor
- July 7 – Seo Woo, Korean actress
- July 9
  - Paweł Korzeniowski, Polish swimmer
  - Cathy Leung, Hong Kong singer
- July 10
  - Mario Gómez, German footballer
  - Park Chu-young South Korean footballer
- July 11
  - Robert Adamson, American actor
  - Adam Gregory, Canadian country music singer and actor
- July 12
  - Emil Hegle Svendsen, Norwegian biathlete
  - Luiz Ejlli, Albanian singer
  - Natasha Poly, Russian model
- July 13
  - Charlotte Dujardin, English dressage rider
  - Guillermo Ochoa, Mexican footballer
- July 14 – Oleksandr Pyatnytsya, Ukrainian javelin thrower
- July 15 – Chris Tiu, Filipino professional basketball player, TV host, commercial model, and politician
- July 16
  - Denis Tahirović, Croatian footballer
  - Yōko Hikasa, Japanese actress

- July 17 – Tom Fletcher, British musician (McFly)
- July 18
    - Chace Crawford, American actor
    - Hopsin, American rapper and record producer
- July 19 – LaMarcus Aldridge, American basketball player
- July 20 – John Francis Daley, American television and film actor
- July 21 – Vanessa Lengies, Canadian actress
- July 22
    - Jessica Abbott, Australian swimmer
    - Ryan Dolan, Irish singer
    - Takudzwa Ngwenya, Zimbabwean-American rugby player
    - Akira Tozawa, Japanese wrestler
- July 23 – Scott Chandler, American football player
- July 24 – Teagan Presley, American porn star
- July 25
    - James Lafferty, American actor and athlete
    - Nelson Piquet Jr., Brazilian Formula One and NASCAR driver
    - Shantel VanSanten, American actress
- July 26 – Leslie Mampe, known as South African American hip hop musician Da L.E.S
- July 27 – Lou Taylor Pucci, American actor
- July 28
    - Dustin Milligan, Canadian actor
    - Darren Murphy, Irish footballer
- July 30
    - Aml Ameen, British actor
    - Elena Gheorghe, Romanian singer and former member of Mandinga

August

Anna Kendrick

Jacqueline Fernandez

Éva Risztov

- August 2 – Britt Nicole (Brittany Nicole Waddell), Christian rock artist

- August 3 – Sonny Bill Williams, New Zealand Rugby League player
- August 4 – Crystal Bowersox, American singer-songwriter
- August 5 – Salomon Kalou, Ivorian footballer
- August 9
  - Anna Kendrick, American actress
  - Hayley Peirsol, American swimmer
- August 10 – Jared Nathan, American actor (d. 2006)
- August 11
  - Asher Roth, American rapper
  - Jacqueline Fernandez, Sri Lankan-born Indian Bollywood actress
- August 14 – Ashlynn Brooke, American pornographic actress
- August 16 – Agnes Bruckner, American actress
- August 21 – Melissa M, French singer
- August 25 – Wynter Gordon, American pop/dance singer-songwriter
- August 27
  - Alexandra Nechita, American artist
  - Kayla Ewell, American actress
  - Sean Foreman, American singer/songwriter and performer; member of electro hop group 3OH!3
- August 28 – Ashlyne Huff, American singer-songwriter and dancer
- August 29 – Jeffrey Licon, American actor
- August 30
  - Eamon Sullivan, Australian swimmer
  - Leisel Jones, Australian swimmer
  - Richard Duffy, Wales international footballer
  - Éva Risztov, Hungarian Olympic Champion swimmer

September

T-pain

Tessanne Chin

Alex Ovechkin

Calvin Johnson

- September 1 – Camile Velasco, Filipina-American actress
- September 2
    - Allison Miller, American actress
    - Yani Gellman, Canadian/Australian film and television actor
- September 3
    - Dominick Cruz, American WEC Bantamweight Champion
    - Brian Stelter, American reporter for NYT
    - Yūki Kaji, Japanese voice actor
    - Yuya Miyashita, Japanese vocalist, actor (Run&Gun)
- September 5 – Dilshad Vadsaria, American television actress
- September 7
    - Alyssa Diaz, American actress
    - Alyona Lanskaya, Belarusian singer
    - Rafinha, Brazilian football player
- September 8 – Denny Morrison, Canadian speed skater
- September 9 – J. R. Smith, American basketball player
- September 10 – Elyse Levesque, Canadian film and television actress
- September 13 – Emi Suzuki, Chinese-born Japanese female model
- September 14 – Aya Ueto, Japanese actress
- September 15 – Iselin Steiro, Norwegian model
- September 16
    - Madeline Zima, American actress
    - Max Minghella, English actor
- September 17
    - Alex Ovechkin, Russian hockey player
    - Jon Walker, American musician (Panic! at the Disco)
    -

- September 21
  - Maryam Hassouni, Dutch actress
  - Lyrian, Japanese moe idol, singer
- September 23
  - Tessanne Chin, Jamaican singer, winner of The Voice season 5
  - Maki Goto, Japanese singer and actress
  - Joba Chamberlain, American baseball player
- September 24
  - Eric Adjetey Anang, Ghanaian sculptor
  - Kimberley Nixon, Welsh actress
  - Jessica Lucas, Canadian actress
- September 26 – Marcin Mroziński, Polish actor, singer and television presenter
- September 28 – Shindong, Korean singer (Super Junior)
- September 29
  - Calvin Johnson, retired American football player
  - Michelle Payne, Australian jockey
  - Dani Pedrosa, Spanish motorcycle racer
- September 30 – T-Pain, American singer-songwriter, rapper, record producer and actor

October

Wayne Rooney

Bruno Mars

Margaret Berger

Hadise

- October 1
  - Tirunesh Dibaba, Ethiopian long distance runner
  - Porcelain Black, American industrial pop singer-songwriter
  - Matt Healy, lead singer and guitarist of the band Rock Incorporated
- October 3
  - Courtney Lee, American basketball player

- Megumi Takamoto, Japanese voice actress and singer
- October 5
  - Brooke Valentine, American singer
  - Nicola Roberts, British singer (Girls Aloud)
- October 7 – Evan Longoria, American professional baseball player
- October 8
  - Kimberly Kevon Williams, American actress
  - Bruno Mars, American singer-songwriter and music producer
  - Magda Apanowicz, Canadian actress
- October 9 – Frankmusik, English electropop musician
- October 10
  - Dominique Cornu, Belgian professional cyclist
  - Aaron Himelstein, American actor
- October 11
  - Margaret Berger, Norwegian electropop singer-songwriter
  - Michelle Trachtenberg, American actress
- October 14
  - Daniel Clark, American-Canadian actor
  - Justin Forsett, American football player
  - Sherlyn, Mexican actress
- October 16 – Casey Stoner, Australian motorcycle racer
- October 17 – Stephanie McIntosh, Irish-Anglo film actor and model
- October 18 – Iori Nomizu, Japanese voce atress, actress and singer
- October 19 – RR Enriquez, Filipino model, television host and actress
- October 20 – Jennifer Freeman, American actress

- October 22
    - Hadise, Belgian singer of Turkish descent
    - Zac Hanson, American musician
    - Manpei Takagi, Japanese actor
    - Shinpei Takagi, Japanese actor
- October 23
    - Masiela Lusha, American author, actress
    - Chris Neal, English footballer
- October 24 – Wayne Rooney, English footballer
- October 25
    - Ciara, African-American singer
    - John Robinson, American actor
- October 26
    - Andrea Bargnani, Italian professional basketball player
    - Asin Thottumkal, Indian actress
- October 27 – Troian Bellisario, American actress

November

Dan Byrd

Carly Rae Jepsen

Kaley Cuoco

- November 2 – Josh Grelle, American voice actor
- November 3
  - Tyler Hansbrough, American basketball player
  - Philipp Tschauner, German footballer
- November 4 – Victoria Leigh Soto, American educator (d. 2012)
- November 5
  - Kate DeAraugo, Australian Idol 2005
  - Elizabeth Rice, American actress
- November 8 – Jack Osbourne, English television personality
-

- November 10
  - Giovonnie Samuels, American actress
  - Ricki-Lee Coulter, former Australian Idol contestant and singer
- November 11
  - Kalan Porter, Canadian singer
  - Raquel Guerra, Portuguese singer and actress
  - Robin Uthappa, Indian cricketer
- November 13
  - Michael Bennett, American football player
  - Asdrúbal Cabrera, Venezuelan baseball player
  - Simo-Pekka Olli, Finnish volleyball player
- November 14 – Thomas Vermaelen, Belgian footballer
- November 15
  - Lily Aldridge, American model
  - Casnel Bushay, Vincentian sprinter
  - Nick Fradiani, American singer
- November 17 – Bea Saw, Filipino actress
- November 20 – Dan Byrd, American actor
- November 21 – Carly Rae Jepsen, Canadian singer-songwriter
- November 22 – Asamoah Gyan, Ghanaian football player
- November 23 – Ahn Hyun-Soo, South Korean short track skater
- November 25 – Marcus Hellner, Swedish cross-country skier
- November 27 – Alison Pill, Canadian actress
- November 28
  - Magdolna Rúzsa, Hungarian singer
  - Ryan Sampson, British actor
- November 30 – Kaley Cuoco, American actress

December

Amanda Seyfried

Raven-Symoné

Edurne

Stephen Dawson

- December 1
  - Philip DeFranco, American YouTube star and video blogger
  - Janelle Monáe, African-American R&B/soul musician
  - Chanel Preston, American porn actress
- December 2 – Amaury Leveaux, French swimmer
- December 3
  - Amanda Seyfried, American actress
  - László Cseh, Hungarian swimmer
- December 4
  - Krista Siegfrids, Finnish singer
  - Stephen Dawson, Irish footballer
- December 5 – Frankie Muniz, American actor, musician, writer, producer, and racecar driver
- December 6 – Dulce María, Mexican actress
- December 7 – Jon Moxley, American professional wrestler
- December 8 – Dwight Howard, American basketball player
- December 9 – Wil Besseling, Dutch golfer
- December 10
  - Raven-Symoné, African-American actress and singer
  - Edmund Entin, American actor
  - Gary Entin, American actor

- o Meghan Linsey, American singer-songwriter, contestant from The Voice season 8
- o Matt Forté, American football player
- December 11 – Samantha Steele, American sportscaster
- December 12 – Juan Camilo Zúñiga, Colombian footballer
- December 14 – Nonami Takizawa, Japanese actress
- December 17 – Greg James, British radio DJ
- December 18 – Hana Soukupová, Czech model
- December 19
  - o Christina Loukas, American diver
  - o Lady Sovereign, British rapper
  - o David Reale, Canadian actor
- December 21
  - o James Stewart Jr., American motorcycle racer
  - o Tom Sturridge, English actor
- December 22 – Edurne, Spanish singer, actress, and TV presenter
- December 23
  - o Harry Judd, English drummer (McFly)
  - o Luke O'Loughlin, Australian actor
- December 26
  - o Yu Shirota, Japanese actor and singer
  - o Beth Behrs, American actress
- December 27 – Paul Stastny, Canadian-American professional ice hockey player
- December 29 – Alexa Ray Joel, American singer, songwriter and pianist
- December 31 – Jonathan Horton, American gymnast

Deaths

January

- January 4 – Sir Brian Horrocks, British general (b. 1895)
- January 5 – Robert L. Surtees, American cinematographer (b. 1906)
- January 13 – Carol Wayne, American actress (b. 1942)
- January 14 – Jetta Goudal, Dutch-born actress (b. 1891)
- January 18 – Mahmoud Mohammed Taha, Sudanese religious thinker (b. 1909)
- January 20 – Gillis W. Long, American politician (b. 1923)
- January 22 – Sir Arthur Bryant, British historian (b. 1899)
- January 29
    - Georges Portmann, French physician. (b. 1890)
    - Billy Cook, Australian jockey (b. 1910)
- January 31 – Tatsuzō Ishikawa, Japanese novelist (b. 1905)

February

- February 4 – Jesse Hibbs, American film director (b. 1906)
- February 6 – Neil McCarthy, British actor (b. 1932)
- February 8 – Marvin Miller, American actor (b. 1913)
- February 11 – Henry Hathaway, American film director (b. 1898)
- February 12 – Nicholas Colasanto, American actor (b. 1924)
- February 18 – Randolph E. Haugan, American author, editor and publisher (b. 1902)
- February 20 – Clarence Nash, American actor (b. 1904)
- February 21
    - Ina Claire, American actress (b. 1893)
    - Louis Hayward, British actor (b. 1909)

- February 22 – Efrem Zimbalist, Russia-born Jewish American violinist (b. 1889)
- February 26 – Tjalling Koopmans, Dutch economist, Nobel Prize laureates (b. 1910)
- February 27
  - Henry Cabot Lodge Jr., American politician (b. 1902)
  - J. Pat O'Malley, English actor (b. 1904)

March

Michael Redgrave

Marc Chagall

- March 3 – Iosif Shklovsky, Soviet astronomer and astrophysicist (b. 1916)
- March 7 – George Schick, Czechoslovakian conductor and music educator (b. 1908)
- March 8 – Edward Andrews, American actor (b. 1914)

- March 10
    - Konstantin Chernenko, Soviet politician (b. 1911)
    - Bob Nieman, American baseball player (b. 1927)
- March 12 – Eugene Ormandy, Hungarian conductor (b. 1899)
- March 13 – Mabel Alvarez, American painter (b. 1891)
- March 16 – Roger Sessions, American composer (b. 1896)
- March 21 – Sir Michael Redgrave, English actor (b. 1908)
- March 23
    - Doctor Richard Beeching, Chairman of British Rail (b. 1913)
    - Zoot Sims, American jazz saxophonist (b. 1925)
- March 28 – Marc Chagall, Russian-born painter (b. 1887)
- March 29 – Jeanine Deckers, Belgian nun and singer (b. 1933)
- March 30 – Shizuko Kasagi, Japanese singer (b. 1914)
- March 31 – Michel Georges-Michel, French painter, journalist, novelist (b. 1883)

April

Enver Hoxha

Tancredo Neves

- April 4 – Kate Roberts (author), Welsh-language authors (b. 1891)
- April 7 – Carl Schmitt, German jurist, political theorist, and professor of law (b. 1888)
- April 8 – J. Fred Coots, American songwriter (b. 1897)
- April 11 – Enver Hoxha, Albanian head of state (b. 1908)
- April 14 – Noele Gordon, British actress (b. 1919)
- April 15 – Jack Medica, American Olympic swimmer (b. 1914)
- April 16 – Scott Brady, American actor (b. 1924)
- April 17 – Evadne Price (aka Helen Zenna Smith), Australian-British writer, actress and astrologer (b. 1888)
- April 18 – Gertrude Caton–Thompson, English archaeologist (b. 1888)
- April 21 – Tancredo Neves, Brazilian elected president (b. 1910)
- April 22 – Paul H. Emmett, American chemical engineer (b. 1900)
- April 23 – Kent Smith, American actor (b. 1907)
- April 25 – Richard Haydn, English actor (b. 1905)

- April 26 – Albert Maltz, American screenwriter, one of the Hollywood Ten (b. 1908)

May

- May 1 – Denise Robins, (aka Francesca Wright, Ashley French, Harriet Gray, Julia Kane) British romance novelist (b. 1897)
- May 4 – Clarence Wiseman, the 10th General of The Salvation Army (b. 1907)
- May 5 – Sir Donald Bailey, British civil engineer (b. 1901)
- May 6
  - Pete Desjardins, American Olympic diver (b. 1907)
  - Julie Vega, Filipino child actress and singer (b. 1968)
- May 7 – Dawn Addams, British actress (b. 1930)
- May 8
  - Theodore Sturgeon, American writer (b. 1918)
  - Dolph Sweet, American actor (b. 1920)
- May 9 – Edmond O'Brien, American actor (b. 1915)
- May 10
  - Tahar Ben Ammar, Tunisian politician (b. 1889)
  - Florizel von Reuter, American violinist and composer (b. 1890)
- May 12 – Jean Dubuffet, French artist (b. 1901)
- May 13
  - Selma Diamond, American actress (b. 1920)
  - Leatrice Joy, American actress (b. 1893)
- May 15 – Rama Devi, leader of nationalists in Orissa. (b. 1889)
- May 16 – Shirley Ximena Hopper Russell, American artist (b. 1886)
- May 17 – Andrej Bicenko, Russian fresco painter. (b. 1886)

- May 19 – W. H. Diddle, American amateur golfer (b. 1882)
- May 22
  - Charles Murphy, American architect. (b. 1890)
  - Franklin Merrell-Wolff, American philosopher. (b. 1887)
- May 30 – George K. Arthur, English actor and producer (b. 1899)

June

- June 1 – Eugène Séguy, French entomologist (b. 1890)
- June 5 – Lord George-Brown, British politician (b. 1914)
- June 6
  - Norman W. Walker, British businessman (b. 1886)
  - Vladimir Jankélévitch, French philosopher and musicologist (b. 1903)
- June 7
  - Georgia Hale, American actress (b. 1905)
  - Gordon Rollings, British actor (b. 1926)
- June 9 – Matsutarō Kawaguchi, Japanese novelist (b. 1899)
- June 10 – George Chandler, American actor (b. 1898)
- June 11 – Karen Ann Quinlan, American right-to-die cause célèbre (b. 1954)
- June 12 – Czesław Marek, Polish composer, pianist (b. 1891)
- June 15 – Percy Fender, English cricketer (b. 1892)
- June 17 – George Jackson, English footballer (b. 1893)
- June 28 – James Craig, American actor (b. 1912)

July

Jan de Quay

Heinrich Böll

- July 2
  - David Purley, British race car driver (b. 1945)
  - Hector Nicol, Scottish entertainer (b. 1920)
- July 4 – Jan de Quay, Dutch politician and psychologist, Prime Minister of the Netherlands (1959–1963) (b. 1901)
- July 8
  - Phil Foster, American actor (b. 1913)
  - Simon Kuznets, American economist (b. 1901)
- July 9 – Jimmy Kinnon, Scottish founder of Narcotics Anonymous (b. 1911)
- July 14 – Lluís Solé, Spanish geographer and academic (b. 1908).
- July 16 – Heinrich Böll, German writer, Nobel Prize laureate (b. 1917)

- July 17 – Margo, Mexican-American actress (b. 1917)
- July 19
    - Janusz A. Zajdel, Polish writer (b. 1938)
    - Louisa Ghijs, Belgian stage actress and wife of Johannes Heesters (b. 1902)
- July 21 – Alvah Cecil Bessie, American screenwriter, one of the Hollywood Ten (b. 1904)
- July 22 – Matti Järvinen, Finnish athlete (b. 1909)
- July 23
    - Kay Kyser, American bandleader (b. 1905)
    - Mickey Shaughnessy, American actor (b. 1920)
- July 25 – Grant Williams, American actor (b. 1931)
- July 26 – Grace Albee, American printmaker and wood engraver. (b. 1890)
- July 27 – John Scarne, American magician and card expert (b. 1903)

August

Louise Brooks

Patrick Barr

- August 2 – Frank Faylen, American actor (b. 1905)
- August 5 – Arnold Horween, Harvard Crimson and NFL football player (b. 1898)
- August 6 – Forbes Burnham, President of Guyana (b. 1923)
- August 8 – Louise Brooks, American actress (b. 1906)
- August 10 – Kenny Baker, American actor and singer (b. 1912)
- August 12
  - Manfred Winkelhock, German race car driver (b. 1951)
  - Kyu Sakamoto, Japanese singer, well known by his most famous song, "Sukiyaki", killed in the crash of Japan Airlines Flight 123 (b. 1941)
- August 14 – Gale Sondergaard, American actor (b. 1899)
- August 15 – Lester Cole, American screenwriter, one of the Hollywood Ten (b. 1904)
- August 22 – Paul Peter Ewald, German-born American crystallographer and physicist (b. 1888)
- August 24 – Morrie Ryskind, American dramatist (b. 1895)
- August 25 – Samantha Smith, American schoolgirl activist (b. 1972)
- August 28 – Ruth Gordon, American actress (b. 1896)

- August 29
  - Evelyn Ankers, British actress (b. 1918)
  - Patrick Barr, British actor (b. 1908)
- August 30 – Taylor Caldwell, Anglo-American writer (b. 1900)
- August 31 – Frank Macfarlane Burnet, Australian biologist, recipient of the Nobel Prize in Physiology or Medicine (b. 1899)

September

John Franklin Enders

Charles Francis Richter

- September 1 – Stefan Bellof, race car driver and 1984 World SportsCars (Group C) Champion (b. 1957)
- September 4
  - Isabel Jeans, British actress (b. 1891)
  - George O'Brien, American actor (b. 1899)

- September 6
  - Isabel Cox-Meighen, wife of Canadian prime minister Arthur Meighen (b. 1882)
  - Little Brother Montgomery, American musician (b. 1906)
- September 7
  - Bruiser Kinard, American football player (Brooklyn Dodgers) and a member of the Pro Football Hall of Fame (b. 1914)
  - Rodney Robert Porter, English biochemist, recipient of the Nobel Prize in Physiology or Medicine (b. 1917)
  - José Zabala-Santos, Filipino cartoonist (b. 1911)
  - George Pólya, Hungarian mathematician (b. 1887)
- September 8 – John Franklin Enders, American scientist, recipient of the Nobel Prize in Physiology or Medicine (b. 1897)
- September 9 – Paul Flory, American chemist, Nobel Prize laureate (b. 1910)
- September 10
  - Ernst Öpik, Estonian astronomer and astrophysicist (b. 1893)
  - Jock Stein, Scottish football player and manager (b. 1922)
- September 11
  - William Alwyn, English composer (b. 1905)
  - Masako Natsume, Japanese actress (b. 1957)
- September 14 – Julian Beck, American actor (b. 1925)
- September 17 – Laura Ashley, Welsh designer (b. 1925)
- September 19 – Italo Calvino, Italian writer (b. 1923)
- September 22 – Axel Springer, German journalist and the founder and owner of the Axel Springer AG (b. 1912)

- September 27 – Lloyd Nolan, American actor (b. 1902)
- September 30
  - Floyd Crosby, American cinematographer (b. 1899)
  - Charles Francis Richter, American seismologist and physicist, creator of the Richter magnitude scale (b. 1900)
  - Simone Signoret, French actress (b. 1921)

October

Rock Hudson

Yul Brynner

Orson Welles

László Bíró

- October 1 – E. B. White, American writer (b. 1899)
- October 2
    - Rock Hudson, American actor (b. 1925)
    - George Savalas, American actor, brother of Telly Savalas (b. 1924)
- October 6 – John W. Snyder, American businessman and Cabinet Secretary (b. 1895)
- October 8 – Nelson Riddle, American bandleader (b. 1921)
- October 10
    - Yul Brynner, American actor (b. 1920)
    - Orson Welles, American film director (b. 1915)
- October 12
    - Johnny Olson, American game show announcer (b. 1910)
    - Ricky Wilson, American guitarist (b. 1953)
- October 14 – Emil Gilels, Soviet pianist (b. 1916)
- October 21
    - Masuiyama Daishirō I, Japanese sumo wrestler (b. 1919)
    - Dan White, American politician and murderer (Moscone–Milk assassinations) (b. 1946)
- October 22 – Thomas Townsend Brown, American inventor (b. 1905)
- October 24 – László Bíró, Hungarian inventor of the ballpoint pen (b. 1899)

- October 25 – Morton Downey, American singer (b. 1901)
- October 29 – John Davis Lodge, American actor and politician (b. 1903)
- October 31 – Poul Reichhardt, Danish actor (b. 1913)

November

- November 1
  - Quick Draw Rick McGraw, American professional wrestler (b. 1955)
  - Ōuchiyama Heikichi, Japanese sumo wrestler (b. 1926)
  - Phil Silvers, American entertainer (b. 1911)
- November 2 – William Lummis, British military historian (b. 1886)
- November 5
  - Spencer W. Kimball, president of The Church of Jesus Christ of Latter-day Saints (b. 1895)
  - Arnold Chikobava, Georgian linguist (b. 1898)
- November 8 – Nicolas Frantz, Luxembourgian cyclist (b. 1899)
- November 9 – Marie-Georges Pascal, French actress (b. 1946)
- November 11 – Pelle Lindbergh, Swedish Professional Hockey goaltender (b. 1959)
- November 13
  - William Pereira, American architect (b. 1909)
  - George Robert Vincent, American sound recording pioneer (b. 1898)
- November 16 – Stuart Chase, American economist (b. 1888)
- November 17
  - Lon Nol, Cambodian general and statesman, Prime Minister and President of Khmer Republic (b. 1913)
  - Jimmy Ritz, American actor (b. 1904)

- November 19 – Stepin Fetchit, American actor (b. 1902)
- November 24 – Big Joe Turner, American blues singer (b. 1911)
- November 25 – Geoffrey Grigson, British poet, writer, critic (b. 1905)
- November 27
  - Fernand Braudel, French historian (b. 1902)
  - Rendra Karno, Indonesian actor (b. 1920)
- November 28 – Johnny McNally, American football player, member of the Pro Football Hall of Fame (b. 1903)

December

Anne Baxter

Ricky Nelson

- December 6
  - Burleigh Grimes, American baseball player (Brooklyn Dodgers) and a member of the MLB Hall of Fame (b. 1893)
  - Burr Tillstrom, American puppeteer (b. 1917)
- December 7
  - Robert Graves, English writer (b. 1895)
  - Potter Stewart, American Supreme Court Justice (b. 1915)
- December 8 – Bill Wambsganss, second baseman in Major League Baseball (b. 1894)
- December 12
  - Anne Baxter, American actress (b. 1923)
  - Ian Stewart, Scottish rock musician (b. 1938)
- December 13 – Paul Caraway, American general and High Commissioner (b. 1905)
- December 14 – Roger Maris, American baseball player (b. 1934)
- December 15 – Carlos Romulo, Filipino diplomat (b. 1899)
- December 16 – William H. Pettit, Christian missionary to Bangladesh (b. 1885)
- December 21 – Kamatari Fujiwara, Japanese actor (b. 1905)
- December 22 – D. Boon, American singer and guitarist (b. 1958)
- December 23
  - Ferhat Abbas, Algerian nationalist (b. 1899)
  - Prince Bira, Prince of Siam and Formula One driver (b. 1914)
- December 24
  - Kouzou Sasaki, Japanese politician (b. 1900)
  - Erich Schaedler, Scottish footballer (b. 1949)

- December 26 – Dian Fossey, American biologist (b. 1932)
- December 27 – Harry Hopman, Australian tennis player and coach (b. 1906)
- December 31
  - Ricky Nelson, American singer and actor (b. 1940)
  - Sam Spiegel, Polish-born film producer (b. 1903)

Date unknown

- Andrej Bicenko, Russian fresco painter and muralist (b. 1886)
- Kaare Bratung, Norwegian cartoonist (b. 1906)
- Hamlet Gonashvili, Georgian singer (b. 1928)

Works of Fiction taking place in 1985

- The 1998 romantic comedy, There's Something about Mary intro is set in 1985. The main character lands a prom date with his crush in High School but is cut short after an embarrassing zipper incident.
- The 1980s sci-fi comedy, Back to the Future takes place in October 1985.

Nobel Prizes

- Physics – Klaus von Klitzing
- Chemistry – Herbert A. Hauptman, Jerome Karle
- Literature – Claude Simon
- Peace – International Physicians for the Prevention of Nuclear War
- Economics – Franco Modigliani
- Nobel Prize in Physiology or Medicine – Michael S. Brown, Joseph L. Goldstein

In the News

TWA Flight 847 is hijacked by Hezbollah.

Terrorist gunman shoot passengers at Rome and Vienna airports.

The British Coal Miners Strike ends and coal mines continue to be closed.

The Greenpeace ship Rainbow Warrior is sunk when French agents plant a bomb on the hull killing Photographer Fernando Pereira.

Mikhail Gorbachev replaces Konstantin Chernenko as Soviet leader.

Live Aid pop concerts in Philadelphia and London raise over 50 million for famine relief in Ethiopia.

Terry Anderson kidnapped in Beirut, Lebanon.

Boris Becker becomes youngest winner at 17 to win the men's Wimbledon championships.

Clive Sinclair launches the Sinclair C5 electric tricycle with a maximum speed of 15mph.

Crowd Violence Erupts during the European Cup Final at Heysel Stadium in Brussels causing a wall to collapse killing 39 football fans.

The space shuttle Atlantis is launched.

Popular Films - Back to the Future, Rambo: First Blood Part II, Rocky IV, The Color Purple, Out of Africa, Cocoon.

1985 Calendar

January 1985
Sun	Mon	Tue	Wed	Thu	Fri	Sat
		1	2	3	4	5
6	7	8	9	10	11	12
13	14	15	16	17	18	19
20	21	22	23	24	25	26
27	28	29	30	31		

February 1985
Sun	Mon	Tue	Wed	Thu	Fri	Sat
					1	2
3	4	5	6	7	8	9
10	11	12	13	14	15	16
17	18	19	20	21	22	23
24	25	26	27	28		

March 1985
Sun	Mon	Tue	Wed	Thu	Fri	Sat
					1	2
3	4	5	6	7	8	9
10	11	12	13	14	15	16
17	18	19	20	21	22	23
24	25	26	27	28	29	30
31						

April 1985
Sun	Mon	Tue	Wed	Thu	Fri	Sat
	1	2	3	4	5	6
7	8	9	10	11	12	13
14	15	16	17	18	19	20
21	22	23	24	25	26	27
28	29	30				

May 1985
Sun	Mon	Tue	Wed	Thu	Fri	Sat
			1	2	3	4
5	6	7	8	9	10	11
12	13	14	15	16	17	18
19	20	21	22	23	24	25
26	27	28	29	30	31	

June 1985
Sun	Mon	Tue	Wed	Thu	Fri	Sat
						1
2	3	4	5	6	7	8
9	10	11	12	13	14	15
16	17	18	19	20	21	22
23	24	25	26	27	28	29
30						

July 1985
Sun	Mon	Tue	Wed	Thu	Fri	Sat
	1	2	3	4	5	6
7	8	9	10	11	12	13
14	15	16	17	18	19	20
21	22	23	24	25	26	27
28	29	30	31			

August 1985
Sun	Mon	Tue	Wed	Thu	Fri	Sat
				1	2	3
4	5	6	7	8	9	10
11	12	13	14	15	16	17
18	19	20	21	22	23	24
25	26	27	28	29	30	31

September 1985
Sun	Mon	Tue	Wed	Thu	Fri	Sat
1	2	3	4	5	6	7
8	9	10	11	12	13	14
15	16	17	18	19	20	21
22	23	24	25	26	27	28
29	30					

October 1985
Sun	Mon	Tue	Wed	Thu	Fri	Sat
		1	2	3	4	5
6	7	8	9	10	11	12
13	14	15	16	17	18	19
20	21	22	23	24	25	26
27	28	29	30	31		

November 1985
Sun	Mon	Tue	Wed	Thu	Fri	Sat
					1	2
3	4	5	6	7	8	9
10	11	12	13	14	15	16
17	18	19	20	21	22	23
24	25	26	27	28	29	30

December 1985
Sun	Mon	Tue	Wed	Thu	Fri	Sat
1	2	3	4	5	6	7
8	9	10	11	12	13	14
15	16	17	18	19	20	21
22	23	24	25	26	27	28
29	30	31				

www.ingramcontent.com/pod-product-compliance
Lightning Source LLC
Chambersburg PA
CBHW060642290526
45793CB00001B/357